The Urbana Free Library

To renew: call 217-367-4057
or go to "*urbanafreelibrary.org*"
and select "Renew/Request Items"

Everyday Mysteries

Where Does the Mail Go?

By Koston Meyer

 Gareth Stevens Publishing

Please visit our website, www.garethstevens.com. For a free color catalog of all our high-quality books, call toll free 1-800-542-2595 or fax 1-877-542-2596.

Library of Congress Cataloging-in-Publication Data

Meyer, Koston.
Where does the mail go? / Koston Meyer.
    p. cm. — (Everyday mysteries)
Includes bibliographical references and index.
ISBN 978-1-4339-6331-5 (pbk.)
ISBN 978-1-4339-6332-2 (6-pack)
ISBN 978-1-4339-6329-2 (library binding)
1. Postal service—United States—Juvenile literature. 2. United States Postal Service—Juvenile literature. I. Title.
HE6371.M625 2011
383'.4973—dc23

                                2011026586

First Edition

Published in 2012 by
Gareth Stevens Publishing
111 East 14th Street, Suite 349
New York, NY 10003

Copyright © 2012 Gareth Stevens Publishing

Designer: Katelyn E. Reynolds
Editor: Greg Roza

Photo credits: Cover, p. 1, 15 (inset) iStockphoto.com; p. 5 Kim Steele/Photodisc/Getty Images; p. 7 Renee Keith/Vetta/Getty Images; p. 9 Sheer Photo, Inc./Photographer's Choice RF/Getty Images; pp. 11, 17, 21, (pp. 3–24 background and graphics) Shutterstock.com; p. 13 Shawn Thew/AFP/Getty Images; p. 15 (main) Robyn Beck/AFP/Getty Images; p. 19 Justin Sullivan/Getty Images.

Printed in the United States of America

CPSIA compliance information: Batch #CW12GS: For further information contact Gareth Stevens, New York, New York at 1-800-542-2595.

Contents

Boldface words appear in the glossary.

Working for the USPS

The US Postal Service (USPS) is our country's mail service. Postal workers help the USPS run smoothly. They have many jobs to do. The post office is open 6 days a week to make sure people across the country get their mail.

mail carrier

5

Addresses and Zip Codes

To mail a letter or **package** to a friend, write their address on the outside. Write your own address on it, too. Addresses include **zip codes**. A zip code tells postal workers what area the mail is going to.

Postage

You must pay **postage** to send mail. Buying stamps pays for postage. Most letters need only one stamp. Packages need more. You can pay a worker at the post office for postage. You can even pay postage online!

In the Mailbox

You might put your mail into a mailbox outside your house. You might use a mailbox on the street. Mail carriers pick up mail from mailboxes. You can also take your mail straight to the post office.

Through the Post Office

Workers at the post office help **customers**. They sell stamps and take your mail. Other workers load mail onto trucks. Many post offices in a large area send their trucks to a building called a mail **processing** plant.

Processing Mail

Machines in a processing plant sort mail by size. They write lines on stamps so the stamps can't be used again. Machines print **bar codes** on mail. Other machines read the bar codes, which help them sort the mail by zip code.

bar code

1
From
0 lbs 4 ozs

FIRST CLASS MAIL

ZIP   DELIVERY CONFIRMATION

Electronic Rate Approved

UNIT
POS

15

Mail on the Go

The sorted mail is put into trays. The trays are put onto trucks. Trucks take the trays to another processing plant close to the zip code the mail is going to. Mail that must go a long way is carried by airplanes.

MAIL ONLY

17

More Processing

At the second processing plant, workers unload the trays. Machines read the bar codes and sort the mail based on where it needs to go. Trucks take the mail to the right post offices. At these post offices, workers prepare the mail for **delivery**.

Out for Delivery

Mail carriers load sorted mail onto mail trucks. They drive to neighborhoods and deliver the mail. Some do it on foot. Mail carriers place mail inside mailboxes. They also pick up mail that's going out—and then the process starts all over again!

20

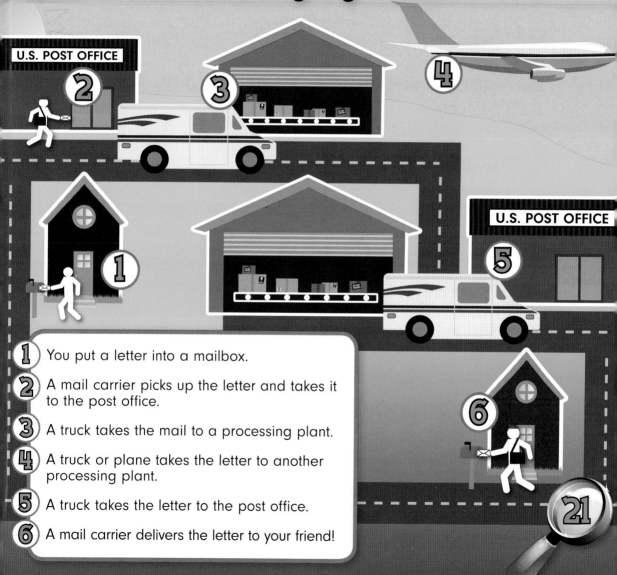

A Journey by Mail!

U.S. POST OFFICE

U.S. POST OFFICE

1. You put a letter into a mailbox.

2. A mail carrier picks up the letter and takes it to the post office.

3. A truck takes the mail to a processing plant.

4. A truck or plane takes the letter to another processing plant.

5. A truck takes the letter to the post office.

6. A mail carrier delivers the letter to your friend!

21

Glossary

bar code: a set of lines that a machine can read

customer: someone who buys goods or services

delivery: the act of taking something to a person or address

package: an object or objects wrapped together or put into a box

postage: money paid to send mail

process: to move something forward in a set of steps. Also, the set of steps itself.

zip code: a set of five or nine numbers added to an address to help sort mail

For More Information

Books

Marsico, Katie. *Working at the Post Office*. Ann Arbor, MI: Cherry Lake Publishing, 2010.

Owen, Ann. *Delivering Your Mail: A Book About Mail Carriers*. Minneapolis, MN: Picture Window Books, 2004.

Somervill, Barbara A. *The History of the Post Office*. Chanhassen, MN: Child's World, 2006.

Websites

How the USPS Works

videos.howstuffworks.com/howstuffworks/71-how-the-usps-works-video.htm

Watch a video showing what happens to your mail after it gets to the post office.

National Postal Museum

postalmuseum.si.edu

Read about the history of the United States Postal Service and learn about stamp collecting.

23

Index